by Grace Hansen

Abdo Kids Jumbo is an Imprint of Abdo Kids
abdobooks.com

abdobooks.com

Published by Abdo Kids, a division of ABDO, P.O. Box 398166, Minneapolis, Minnesota 55439.

Abdo Kids Jumbo™ is a trademark and logo of Abdo Kids.

Printed in China

052019

092019

Photo Credits: Alamy, iStock, Shutterstock

Production Contributors: Teddy Borth, Jennie Forsberg, Grace Hansen
Design Contributors: Dorothy Toth, Pakou Moua

Library of Congress Control Number: 2018963577

Publisher's Cataloging-in-Publication Data

Names: Hansen, Grace, author.

Title: Egypt / by Grace Hansen.

Description: Minneapolis, Minnesota : Abdo Kids, 2020 | Series: Countries | Includes online resources and index.

Identifiers: ISBN 9781532185502 (lib. bdg.) | ISBN 9781532186486 (ebook) | ISBN 9781532186974 (Read-to-me ebook)

Subjects: LCSH: Egypt--Juvenile literature. | Egypt--History--Juvenile literature. | Africa--Juvenile literature. | Geography--Juvenile literature.

Classification: DDC 962--dc23

Table of Contents

Egypt

Egypt is a country in Africa.

A small part of it is in Asia too.

Europe
Mediterranean Sea
Asia
Egypt
Atlantic
Ocean
Red Sea
Africa
N
W
E
S

More than 99 million people live in Egypt. Cairo is the country's largest city. It is also the capital!

Egypt's History

Egypt has a very long and interesting history. It was one of the first **civilizations**. Ancient Egypt was ruled by pharaohs for 3,000 years.

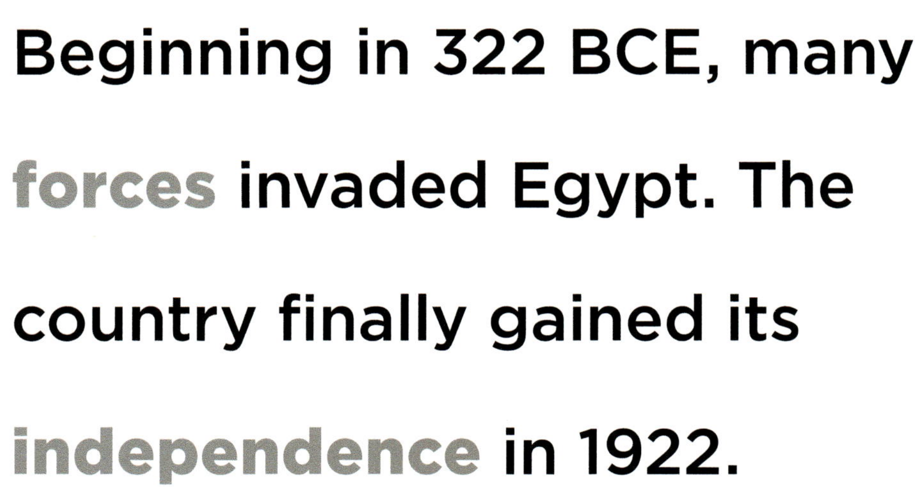

Beginning in 322 BCE, many **forces** invaded Egypt. The country finally gained its **independence** in 1922.

Geography

Desert covers much of Egypt. The Sahara Desert covers 31% of Africa. Almost all of Egypt is a part of the Sahara.

The Nile River flows 1,000 miles (1,609 km) through Egypt. It empties into the Mediterranean Sea. Most Egyptians live near the river. There the land is **arable**.

15

Plants & Animals

Crocodiles can be found in the Nile River. Papyrus grows along its banks. Ancient Egyptians used this plant to make **scrolls**, boats, and sandals.

The Pyramids

Egypt has everything from modern cities to ancient pyramids. Pyramids are giant tombs for pharaohs. Egypt's most famous pyramids are found in Giza.

The Great Pyramid of Giza is the tomb of Khufu. He was a pharaoh who ruled more than 4,500 years ago. The tomb is made from about 2.3 million blocks.

Awesome Landmarks in Egypt

Abu Simbel Temples
Aswan Governorate, Egypt

The Great Sphinx
Giza, Egypt

Suez Canal
Waterway connecting the Mediterranean Sea to the Red Sea

White Desert
Farafra, Egypt

Glossary

arable – capable of being farmed.

civilization – an advanced stage (as in art, science, and government) of development of a society.

force – a group that uses violence or power to control or attempt to control another group.

independence – freedom from outside control.

scroll – a roll of paper or parchment used to write on.

Index

Visit abdokids.com to access crafts, games, videos, and more!

Use Abdo Kids code **CEK5502** or scan this QR code!